With words of affection, "I realized just how much / I run through your veins" – *Thomas at 13* – and words of loss, "But today my heart is hurting, / Because part of it is missing" – *11/16/00 (Coping #2)* – Mark Pottorff draws you into this collection and *Around That Old Table,* where conversations with loved ones, here and gone, become conversations with the reader as he shares his love and respect for family and tradition.

-Ken Gierke, author of *Random Riffs* and *Heron Spirit*

Mark's spirit conveys the loving sort of haunting that I grew up hearing about in tales of guardian angels. His use of imagery, line breaks, and pacing bakes emphasis into the sacred spaces between words. The elegance of Mark's elegies reminds readers to look to their loved ones, memorize their faces while you can, and keep them alive in the blanket of each breath. For those of us who have never lived in the layered embrace of genuine generations, he introduces a rich vein of humanity, this haunting love a Dadly reminder of who we are, and could be, together.

> -Jon Freeland, *Lost Eel Questions* (Stubborn Mule Press)

Mark Pottorff writes about what is important to him. His poetry tells you who he is. It is well crafted, emotional and mature but not angry. It feels like looking in the mirror. An important work that will touch your soul. It will cause you to examine your emotions and life in general.

> -John Clayton, *Cutting Words*

Around That Old Table

Poems by Mark Pottorff

Spartan
Press

Spartan Press
Kansas City, Missouri

Spartan
Press

Copyright © Mark Pottorff, 2026
First edition 1 3 5 7 9 10 8 6 4 2
ISBN: 979-8-89975-029-8
LCCN: 2026932414

Author photo: Rachel J. Hays

Acknowledgments:

Thank you to the Gumbo Bottoms Single Pot Still Poetry Society and the Osage Arts Community. Their support of poets' work has helped drive me to write and to take the initiative to seek publication.

Thank you also to Jason Ryberg for giving me the final push to put my work out there for the world to see.

Table of Contents

For my wife, Patty, our children, and all my family who have held me together for so long. Also for my Gumbo Bottoms Single Pot Still Poets Society family, because, as I learned long ago, family is not always blood.

"You go through life wondering what is it all about, but at the end of the day, it's all about family."

-Rod Stewart

Saplings, Branches, Trees

The older generation fades;
Now my parents, once the young ones,
Fill the void. I and my
Siblings, always the youth before,
Become the parents.

Sapling becomes tree; tree
Bears forth branches; branches
Bear fruit. Fruit brings forth
Seed, and seed becomes sapling.

So the cycle follows. One
Begets the other and around
Again. The parent once the child;
The child once the babe, and the
Babe now the grandparent.

To Grandpa

I walked down the worn path
That was so familiar to us
And talked to you as I went.
I talked of days spent with
You fixing fence in the cow pasture
And of funny stories you told.
I talked of Grandma and Mom,
Aunt Mary, and Aunt Dorothy. I talked
Of Steve, and Homer, and Clayton.
I rambled on of days gone before
Until I could ramble no more.

Then,
I cried. I cried because I could
Talk no more and because you would
Talk no more. And I cried because
You were gone.

Almost Gone

You broke a young boy's
Heart more than once with
Your little mood swings, but
Nothing compared to the day
You didn't return. Your
Silly scene for attention back-
Fired, and your ultimatum
Was challenged, leaving you
No choice but to not come home.

Your determination left
Us behind and left a teenager
Broken and angry. His memories
Of the fun shared with you could
Carry him only so far. In the end,
They were what saved his love for you,
But you made it hard.

When you finalized the divorce,
I stopped talking about you and
Shut you out the best my brain

Could. When Grandpa died,
Mama said she was an orphan, but
You were still out there.

You've come back to us now,
And Mom's no longer an orphan.
The harsh memories of those years
Still invade sometimes, but
The hurt has faded, almost gone.

I Will Not Grieve

I will not grieve him until
He is dead.
He will eventually succumb to you,
Perhaps tomorrow, perhaps a year of tomorrows,
But I will not grieve for him
Until he is dead.

I will check the cows as many
Times as he wishes; I will
Sit on the front patio when we
Visit, but I will not grieve for him
Until he is dead.

Those who think they know can
Surmise how little time he has left,
But I will not grieve for him
Until he is dead.

I will talk of Walter, Bob, Virgil,
May, Opal, Martha, and any others
Until I am blue in the face.

I will listen to the same story a
Thousand times if need be,
But I will not grieve for him
Until he is dead.

I will try to know all his mannerisms and
I will help my children get to know him as
Well they can in the time they are with
Him, but I will not grieve for him
Until he is dead.

When that day has come, grief will
Walk by my side, and I will
Mourn. But I will not grieve for him
Until he is dead.

Around That Old Table

As we sat around that old table
The next day and searched boxes
For pictures to set beside the casket,
Dee came with snapshots taken just the
Past few years. We looked at each
One, and she stated, "Look how Lee is always
Reaching out to touch your mother."

Then my mind went back, back to another
Time. I remembered the radio, one of those
Old country songs, and you hurrying
Playfully into the kitchen to drag Mom
From the hamburgers she was frying to
Dance her around the room. She, protesting the
Whole time, loved it.

I saw Mom stopped halfway in her trip
Across the living room as you grabbed
Her hand, pulled her to you, and held her
Close, as you sang a chorus of "Give Me
Forty Acres to Turn This Rig Around."

You'd sing your chorus, kiss her, and
Let her go, as you went back to your work.

Back at that old table, I remembered last night.
As pain gripped your body and you slipped deeper
Away from us, your hands, as though by heavenly
Decree, reached out to hold Mom near. You
Grasped her arm as one trying to hold on to
Forty-one years of love for one brief moment,
As always, reaching out to touch our mother.

Ghosts

Last night I stood at the sink
Doing some mindless task,
As my thoughts passed through
A series of questions I had.
Without allowing time for
Logic, I told myself to
Ask Dad about it – then ...
I remembered that Dad is
Dead.

Then tonight I sat at another
Highschool ballgame when
Across the way sat Dad.
The straw hat, thin face, sharp
Nose, and long sleeved, cotton
Shirt defied the fact that he
Died a year ago last month.

My mind knew the truth,
But my heart still panicked
(and rejoiced)

At the thought that he was there.
My ghost brought me comfort while
My heart thumped in despair.

11/16/00
(Coping #2)

I.

Today my heart is hurting,
Not because of blockage a doctor
Could remove with a knife, but
Because part of it is missing.

And though I know the memories
Rush to fill the spot her loss
Has left void, memories are but
Mere shadows, lacking the balm
I need to sooth this pain.

And though others are in my heart
To help ease the pain, still
The hurt exists. It will lessen
With time, but it is real.

II.

And now, at thirty-five years,
An orphan. I must again
Learn that I can turn elsewhere
To find that solace she provided.

It will, in coming seasons, be easier
To turn to others (although it will
Lack something only Mom could give),
But today my heart is hurting,
Because part of it is missing.

As Her Tired Soul Sat

As her tired soul sat
Before her daughter's coffin,
I knew she was resurrecting
Pain she had lay to rest
In a hidden corner of her heart
Over these past forty-some years.

She sat lifeless and let
Each of us hug and kiss --
Say, "I love you, Grandma." -- and
Try to console her through pain
We could not begin to understand.

She sat, reached out a hand
To say what it was she could to
Her baby lying before her, then
Let us roll her back out the
Door to the waiting van that
Would take her tired soul back
To her lonely bed and small room.

And, These Six

Now, two and something years later,
We return again to this hill --
Four who were here before,
The nephew who was more the son,
And she, who came to carry her mother home.
We again come to this, the resting place of our
Ancestors, the place we come for
Our past and strength, and we prepare
To carry her once as she has carried
Us so many times. Cristin, like his
Father before him, says, "This end
First and then right into the tent."
We, as with our father before,
Take a breath and lift our load;
Then, we six bear Mom to her grave.

Sale Bills

Forty-two years together and,
It seems, summed up in
Two short lists in a small
Sale bill in the local Sunday paper.
But these lines labeled: antiques,
And equipment, and furniture, and ...
Only show a minor piece of the
Existence they had in their years.
There is no place to list the
Children (I doubt we could get
Much for us), and there is no
Place to list the grandchildren
(but they are priceless – don't bother).
There is no place to list our
Memories (but they are too precious,
I'll not part with them), memories
Of car trips, singing "Church in the Vale,"
And of camping under the bridge all
Those years ago. There is no place
To list a heritage passed from their

Parents and on down to us and on
Down, yet again, to our children.
There is no place to list two lives
That ended too soon but continue
In those left behind. No place
To list them, so I will just hold
Them close to my heart, never sold.

10/16/01

Until that little newsbreak come on,
I had not thought about what day it was.
It had glanced across my mind briefly
Last week when I had looked at the
Calendar, but today, I had not really
Allowed myself the time to think.
But then, in front of that old
Philco, it came to me what day it was.
It was all there again:
A week of her feeling bad, a week
Of her in the hospital, and a week
In hell as we set the dates, chose the
Pall bearers, got the details in order,
Lay her to her final rest, and
Read the last will and testament,
But I had not thought about what day it was,
Until that little newsbreak came on.

First Time

Standing in the middle of the hay field,
My dad said, "Go get my tools,"
And I, being the young fool I was, started to walk.
"No, take the truck" was the gruff comeback.

My slight protest went unheeded, despite
The fact that I had never been behind the wheel.
"You can do it; just take your time," was his
Advice, and I climbed into the cab of nowhere.

With my knees shaking and gears grinding, I slowly
Made my way to the tools on the other end.
I then climbed confidently back in and drove to
Dad. "Didn't take long, so it couldn't have hurt much,"

Was
All
He
Said.

Need

Stand --
Call my name,
Feel my touch.

Scream --
Wake from sleep,
Feel my touch.

Smile --
Show your desire,
Feel my touch.

Lay --
Touch my hand,
Feel my need.

Tracings

Gently trace your name
In the tender of my back
And mark me as your own.
Then, soothe the edges
Of my spastic world,
Keeping me close to your
Heart to feel the rhythm.
Gently caress my life
With the fingers of your
Soul and hold me to your
Bosom, safe and warm.

Loving You

I run my fingers across
Your petal soft back and
Trace "I Love You" up
The trail of your spine.

I pray a little prayer,
A silent recognition to
God for you, your love,
And the love I have to give.

They are all gifts He has
Given me, or really us,
To cherish and hold near
When all else seems to go wrong.

I get up and write some
Lines that can never be
Enough to tell you how
I feel on this quiet night.

You sigh, still asleep,
And, without knowing it, call
Me back to your side, to
Our bed, to your waiting love.

Interview With a Dinosaur

One by one she lines
The stuffed toys so
Each one has a front
Row seat for the show
Then, in a flash of extravagance,
The emcee, that she has now
Become, emerges to announce,
"Ladies and gentlemen, boys and
Girls, BARNEY!"
Each little member of
The audience responds
In the proper manner,
So she moves on to the personal
Interviews, "Now, dinosaur,
What's your name?"

Thomas at 13

I stood in the hallway
And listened as you
Sang along with Haggard.
I heard how you matched
His tones and notes
And how you seemed to
Imitate his style of singing,
And as I listened to your
Interpretation of his song,
I realized just how much
I run through your veins.

Mom

I stood in the darkness tonight,
Listening to the tree frogs,
And it took me back, back
To those days so long along ago.

To days when you where there,
Calling me back in from the pastures,
Telling me to play one more game,
Urging me to let the dogs alone.

I recall the honks from the horn,
Three long, two short, and then
Home we came. I recall you
And Dee telling us to be careful and
Then hoping we would come back in
One piece. You recognized our youth
But hoped we had the sense to
Live through it and to learn from it.

Those frogs took me back, and
Made me remember, thinking of my
Time with you and all those who
Made me who I am, and
Then I smiled.

Dad's Wild Rose

That wild rose in our backyard
Blooms each spring, just in time
To remember your birthday.
It's not the one you dug for my
Young wife before your passing
(That one is still at our old house
In Sedalia where I planted it.).

I planted this one a few years after
We bought this house, after she had
Asked me to do it a few times. It was
Your voice in the back of my head that
Finally pushed me to put a shovel in the
Ground, and though you were gone twenty years
Before I dug it, I still call it your wild rose.

On The Eve of My 60th Birthday

It is one hour and 18 minutes
Until I turn 60 years old, and
Yes, I am as surprised as you are that I
Am here to mark this auspicious,
Albeit surprising, occasion.

I lie in this bed, as you sleep
Beside me, and I know fully well
That you are the reason I have
Survived. Know too that I will do
Anything to keep you safe.

So, sleep well and know I
Am yours, because I know
I am yours.

Dear Mitch

As I held our father's hand
And knew he was passing,
I felt a pang of regret that
This was the first time,
In my adult life, I had
Told him, "I love you, Dad."

I had never, in the years
I have been with Patty,
Had a problem telling her
Or our kids how I felt.
I told them daily, even multiple
Times, "I love you," but I
Had not said it to Dad.

At that point, I decided
I would not make the
Same mistake with Mom.
So, now, each time I leave
Her house, I try to remember

To say, "I love you, Mom."
I give a simple kiss and these
Few words as a little assurance
In my absence from her.

Then, seeing you on that bed,
Collar around your neck and
Blood streaming down your
Tattered face, I felt the same
Fear of loss I felt with Dad.
Yet, as Mom drove you away
From the emergency door, I
Could not, out of some senseless
Macho stupidity (or something),
Tell you what I was thinking.
Instead, I said, "Be careful."

What I meant to say was a
Simple, "I love you, brother."

Mark Pottorff is a retired public educator, who taught H.S. English for ten years before going over to the dark side to become an administrator. Two constants in his life have been family and poetry, and the former is heavily reflected in the latter. His free verse poetry often embodies the human battle between the need to express and release our tenderest moments and the societal pressure to keep it all in as we process the trauma of our lives.

This project was made possible, in part, by generous support from the Osage Arts Community.

Osage Arts Community provides temporary time, space and support for the creation of new artistic works in a retreat format, serving creative people of all kinds — visual artists, composers, poets, fiction and nonfiction writers. Located on a 152-acre farm in an isolated rural mountainside setting in Central Missouri and bordered by ¾ of a mile of the Gasconade River, OAC provides residencies to those working alone, as well as welcoming collaborative teams, offering living space and workspace in a country environment to emerging and mid-career artists. For more information, visit us at www.osageac.org

Osage Arts Community